Meerbott's Fables

*Stories, Questions & Coloring Pages
for a New Generation of Adults*

VOLUME I

Kelly Meerbott

kardia
WRITING & PUBLISHING

Meerbott's Fables / Kelly Meerbott—1st ed.

ISBN Paperback: 978-1-956989-24-3
ISBN Hardcover: 978-1-956989-25-0

Contents

Preface

A fable is a fictional narrative meant to teach a moral lesson. The characters in a fable are usually animals whose words and actions reflect human behavior. A form of folk literature, the word fable comes from the Latin meaning "to speak."

This collection of fables is based on 30+ years of intentional observation, personal experience, client experiences, and more than eleven years of working in corporate America.

Introduction

We are living in a time where we are at war with accountability and civility, and are in danger of cutting ourselves off from learning and innovation. We've limited our worldview to the way that we singularly choose to see and experience the world, rather than remaining open to its true vast and diverse nature. The world is tumultuous and we are at a tipping point of losing our humanity. In the words of *The New York Times* best-selling author, activist, thought-leader, spoken word artist, and founder of *The Body is Not An Apology* global movement Sonya Renee Taylor, "We are being given the opportunity to stitch a new garment. One that fits all of humanity and nature."

Recently, we lost our five-year-and-nine-month-old golden retriever, Karly Love to Lyme disease. We are dedicated and dutiful pet owners. This disease is insidious and came out of nowhere. We did everything we could to save her life. In the end, the most compassionate thing we could do for our little girl was to help her transition over the "rainbow bridge." We said our goodbyes on January 18, 2023.

Since that moment in time, in addition to grieving Karly, I've been thinking about the lessons I've learned from her during the brief time we had with her.

She was the embodiment of love on four paws. Much like a little kid, she saw the world through the lens of wonder, play, and love. Karly never took herself too seriously and wasn't afraid to ask for what she wanted, whether it was a scratch, a walk, a cuddle, or just to be with you.

The natural world has a lot to teach us, and our companion animals are a reflection of our connection to nature as a whole.

It is my intention that this book of fables leverages lessons from nature, my experience, and my imagination to help you ask yourself where change for the better is possible. To question what we think we know and to ask ourselves what needs to shift or change within ourselves to make the world a better place.

Acknowledgment

I'd like to thank the connection to the source bigger than myself. These stories came through me like a divine channel. It is my intention that they fall on people's hearts and create positive change.

To my soulmate and love of my life, Brian Meerbott. You have been with me through thick and thin. You taught me that true love will never make you question yourself or what's real. Thank you for seeing me. Thank you for supporting me. Thank you for loving me even when it was tough.

Thank you to Jasmine, Murphy, Karly Love, Pablo Escobar, Tessie Lynn, and Tallulah "Tully" Rose. You have all been incredible companions and friends, and consistently demonstrated what unconditional love looks like. You have all left indelible pawprints on my heart that will last a lifetime. To the new companion animals yet to come into my life...I look forward to meeting you.

To the Deluxe Get It Done book team — this book would not have come to life without you. You held space, created accountability, and breathed life into my vision for this book of fables. The depth of my gratitude to you far exceeds words.

Specifically to Lindsey, Winnie Cooper, Alex, Zuki, Woz, Olive Pants, Penguin, Willa, Andrw, Ori, Nebula, Nova, Lucy, Tracie, and Jeffery.

To my family, specifically to my mother, Irene. The idea of "Midas the Mouse" came from you. You taught me how to tell powerfully visual stories and how they can positively impact an audience. Thank you for that.

To my bonus family (The Meerbotts), you are the gift I got from the union with Brian. You are a wonderful group of humans who have welcomed me with open arms and made me feel like family from the first introduction. I appreciate all of you.

To "The Coven" - Cari, Lexie & Marci and my other inner circle friends (you know who you are), I'm grateful we found each other. True friends are hard to come by, and I don't take that lightly.

To my team at YOU: Loud & Clear, Inc., Cecily, Jesmae, Laura, Nicole, Gayle, Sharon, and Dan. What a group! You are each a valuable part of this journey and I couldn't have done this without you.

To Ernest Owens, friend, colleague, editor and purveyor of truth, your wisdom, humor, and insight have been gifts to me and humanity. Thank you for being part of my journey.

The Turtle and the Light

LEATHERBACK SEA TURTLES
Dermochelys coriacea

Once upon a time, in the deep waters of the Pacific Ocean, where no fishing boat could reach to destroy their peaceful family, Max and Myrtle Turtle were preparing for Myrtle's 10,000-mile swim to get to her annual nesting grounds.

Yes, Myrtle was pregnant again. She was excited but knew she had a long journey to reach her safe space to give birth. The excitement of meeting her newborns propelled her forward and fueled her. Myrtle knew she had to return to the region to make her nest—located on the east coast of Florida, right near Boynton Beach, about an hour north of Miami.

While she loved Miami's culture, flair, music, art, and vibrant colors, the sensory overload was a little too much for her to give birth to their children peacefully. There was also the traffic to contend with—one of the biggest killers of baby turtles. Myrtle had a precise birth plan with many contingencies.

So, Myrtle kissed Max, said her goodbyes, and left their 4000-foot-deep home to begin the journey to South Florida.

Myrtle swam non-stop for day, floating in safe areas to sleep or rest briefly. At 2 a.m. on a Wednesday, she finally reached the warm waters of the east coast of Florida.

"Perfect," Myrtle thought, "no one is on the beach." She felt her way up the ridge of the bluffs in the dark. She sniffed around and felt the wind push the scent of where she had previously made her nest, where her babies hatched yearly.

Myrtle knew she had ten times to get it right because only one or two of her thousands of babies would make it to adulthood. Her babies were not only vulnerable to extinction as leatherbacks, but they also had only two months after they were born to make the 10,000-mile journey back to their home in the Pacific Ocean.

Leatherback Turtles could trace their lineage back to the days of the dinosaurs. Yet, they had to contend with threats on nesting beaches, including the coastal developers who cared solely about building new, higher, flashier condos with high rents to line their pockets.

Still, she knew there were the egg collectors who would dig through her nest, pick out the best eggs, and destroy the rest. There were human and animal predators; raccoons and dogs would eat her eggs. People who didn't turn off their cell phone lights or vehicle headlights would lure her babies into fatal situations. And if her offspring made a wrong left turn into a sandcastle disaster could ensue—she had seen her daughters and sons walk confidently toward the light of the water and fall headfirst into a ditch of a sandcastle, break their necks, and die instantly. She also watched her babies choke on plastic straws, which they mistook for food. This fact was painful for Myrtle, and she pushed the thought away, "I'll think about that later." She had come to peace with this sad part of her life.

With all these challenges, Myrtle was hopeful that maybe four out of her 1,000 babies this year would make it. She used her fins to dig her hole and settle down to lay her first clutch of 100 eggs. Myrtle relaxed to the soft sound of the waves crashing against the sand. She lifted her head and sniffed the salt air, feeling comforted that she had been born here.

She knew that this was the best chance for her babies to make it. That, and hope that the humans who occupy the same space would turn off their cell phones, turn off their headlights, and dispose of their garbage properly. Myrtle finished giving birth to her first clutch of eggs this year, backed up, and covered them tightly in the sand. She kissed one of her front fins, patted the mound, and whispered a silent prayer, hoping all of them would survive.

The birth process went on for the next ten days. Each night, Myrtle would find a spot to give birth to her 100 eggs and then move on. Finally, exhausted ten days later, she left and headed back to her husband.

After two months of incubation, the hatchlings began to emerge from their nest and enter the water to start their journey towards adulthood. Their eyes began to open, and their eggshells began to crack.

One headstrong baby male turtle was confused when he finally broke through the sand into the night air. Disoriented, he didn't know where to go. But he had ancient wisdom infused into his DNA and knew which direction to head. As his brothers and sisters headed in the opposite direction, he tried to encourage them and said, "No, no, use your eyes. Use your ears. Use your noses. Don't you hear the waves crashing to the left, not right? Can't you smell the salt air?"

But his brothers and sisters had other ideas. Collectively they looked at him and said, "No. You need to head towards the light with us. Come on, brother. We can all make it together," as they headed in the opposite direction.

Shaking his head. He knew that was not right, so he decided to go his own way and name himself Marley. He knew once he entered the water as a male leatherback turtle, he never had to come out of the water again.

He followed his gut, crawling towards the sound of the crashing waves and the salt-air smell. Moments later, he heard a terrible crash and horns honking as he realized that the he lost the other 99 members of his clutch.

Shocked, he absorbed the trauma of watching his 99 brothers and sisters die. This determined turtle baby was intelligent and intuitive and knew his name was Marley. Nobody told him his name was Marley, and he simply knew it.

Marley witnessed the other nine clutches of his brothers and sisters begin to hatch in the Florida moonlight. He called out to them, "Come this way! We'll all go into the water together, and we'll find mom and dad. I know the way," shouted Marley.

"How do you know the way?" his new brothers and sisters asked.

"I just know. You must trust me. It's in our DNA, generations in the making."

"You have no way of knowing, you're only minutes old," they said. "We're going to go towards the light."

"Don't go towards the light," pleaded Marley. "I saw our brothers and sisters killed by an 18-wheeler truck."

"No, this is the direction we're going to go."

He wiped big turtle tears from his eyes and watched as the second set of his brothers and sisters headed towards a new light, not the same as the headlights he saw before, but a little bit smaller. Then he saw it happen. A human with a cell phone flashlight snatched up the turtle babies for their meat and decoration.

As his brothers and sisters screamed, he backed closer and closer to the water.

Marley knew that he loved his siblings, but his survival was his sole focus. He continued to move towards the water as the remaining eight clutches of his brothers and sisters died by coastal developers, raccoons, dogs, people harvesting eggs for food, or other people collecting eggs. He even saw dogs and raccoons working together to destroy a nest.

Marley couldn't handle any more trauma. He headed towards the water, gliding into the cool surf. He began to swim. It was second nature, and Marley instinctively knew which way to go. The infant leatherback began to distinguish between plastic debris and jellyfish.

"Ohhhh, jellyfish," Marley thought, "they're delicious."

After two weeks of non-stop swimming, he made it to his home and met his mom and dad for the first time.

"Son, we're so glad to meet you!" they said in unison. "How did you survive the journey?"

"I trusted my gut," said Marley. "And I didn't follow the crowd. But, mom and dad, unfortunately, my remaining 999 brothers and sisters didn't make it. I tried to save them, but they wouldn't listen. Instead, I saved myself."

Max and Myrtle embraced Marley. Their leatherback hug comforted him. Myrtle whispered in Marley's ear, "Son, the first turtle you need to take care of is yourself, and that's what you did." Max continued, "We couldn't be prouder that you trusted your intuition, didn't follow the crowd, and came home safe to us."

THE END

THE MORAL

Forging your own path has the potential to save your life.

THREE QUESTIONS

What do you want in life?

_____

_____

_____

_____

_____

Why do you want that specific thing?

_____

_____

_____

_____

How do you want to be remembered when you die?

_____

_____

_____

_____

II

The Seahorse Father

LONGSNOUT SEAHORSES

Hippocampus reidi

Once upon a time, Stuart and Sheryl Seahorse were pregnant. After four rounds of painful IVF, they were successfully able to lay eggs in Stuart's specialized pouch on his abdomen.

The first two rounds were unsuccessful because Sheryl's body didn't respond positively to the hormones that Dr. C. Horse kept injecting into her.

Because Stuart could not camouflage his body to avoid predation, a predator snuck up on him twice and ate the eggs.

Round five, Stuart incubated the babies again, and Sheryl successfully laid them in his specialized pouch. He limited his movements to a protected area in mangrove roots, where he could hide and keep the babies safe until birth. Every day he would go to the forest and attach himself to the mangroves until he had to work at the plankton factory.

Sheryl was the head of the National Seahorse Commission (NSC) and commuted to work via the current daily. It became Stuart's responsibility to protect their babies, while working at the plankton factory. A risky task, indeed.

He noticed a shift in attitude towards him as soon as he came into work with his big pregnant belly. Management began to treat him differently. At first, it was subtle; a glance at his stomach or a roll of their eyes. Then it became blatant.

Managers saying things like, "Oh, after the babies are born, can we expect you at work?"

One of Stuart's female supervisors, who had been with him through the painful four pregnancies they lost, tried to renegotiate his paternity leave—piecing together options that benefited the company. She tried to take away parts of Stuart's leave to fit what she felt was best for the plankton factory. All while he was preparing for the arrival of his 2,000 babies.

Because Stuart was incubating these 2,000 eggs, he rarely had the energy to argue with his supervisors over his paternity leave. But he knew that his incubation period was rapidly coming to an end.

He cited that Amazon, Netflix, the US Military, and Microsoft, those "human companies," had agreed that paternity leave brought great employee satisfaction to their organizations. His supervisors looked down their snouts at Stuart and said, "That's a human for you. Messing everything up when it should just be left alone! And by the way, Stuart, 71% of organizations in the human world are still not offering paternity leave."

The plankton factory offered paternity leave. However, Stuart felt pressured not to take it, as leadership was communicating with him through coercive memos with passive aggressive statements.

He had seen some new dads that worked at the plankton factory be fired, demoted, and lose promotions for taking their paternity leave. Stuart witnessed one of his colleagues quitting after his supervisor said, "You have six weeks of paternity leave, but you're not taking any. We need you to get this big order out."

Another executive in another factory told Stuart that her husband's boss had criticized him by asking, "Why isn't your wife taking maternity leave? She's the mother, isn't she? Isn't it the female's job to raise the kids?"

Stuart kept his snout to the grindstone. He completed his work and returned home to the mangrove roots, where he softly caressed his belly and hummed lullabies to the babies.

Sheryl came home from work at the NSC. As a couple, they discussed the stresses of their day.

"How did it go today, love?" Sheryl asked.

Shocked and depressed, Stuart shook his head, "I'm bumping up against stereotypes and programming. 73% of fathers in the plankton factory say they have little workplace support. 21% of my colleagues in the company fear losing their jobs if they take full paternity leave."

"Well," said Sheryl, "we're still held back by those who uphold traditions that humans impressed upon our culture. One, that men are the primary breadwinners and two, that women are the primary caregivers for the children. Both are obstacles to our professional growth and the survival of our family."

Stuart nodded his head in agreement. "I know how hard you've worked for your position, and we've both worked hard to have our children. We'll do everything we can to ensure these babies survive and thrive."

Sheryl smiled and added, "Fortunately, we don't have the financial restrictions other couples have."

"Right," said Stuart, "but it just doesn't seem fair that women are required to incubate the babies. When really, that's our job as fathers, and we want to do it and participate in the birth process."

Sheryl, moved by her husband's love and dedication, said, "I know you do, honey. Let's keep thinking about it. I'm sure there's a solution that would create a win-win for everyone involved."

As the birth date came closer and closer, Stuart felt his body adjusting to the growing 2,000 babies in his belly. At 3 a.m. one morning, his belly began to rumble, and 2,000 babies burst into the world. It almost looked like his belly was exploding.

"Sheryl. Look at them all. Aren't they beautiful?"

"Yes," Sheryl cried. "Stuart, you did a wonderful job. Now we have 2,000 little ones that need our love and care. And since I haven't taken the first week of my maternity leave. I can take the first shift," she said.

Stuart left his newborns and went to the plankton factory. While on the line, his mind kept drifting back to Sheryl at home with their new babies. He auto-piloted his way through exhaustion and fatigue, until he couldn't take it anymore.

He went to his supervisor again.

"Listen, I gave birth to 2000 babies, five hours ago."

"Congratulations to you and Sheryl," she said.

"Thanks," Stuart said. "I'd like to take my paternity leave."

"Well, that's not going to be possible, Stuart," she said. "We have a huge order for plankton for the NSC Convention in the next couple of weeks. If you want to take time off, you'll have to wait until those two weeks are up."

"My wife's the head of the NSC. Let me talk to her," said Stuart.

"Yeah, talk to her about possibly leaving her job and staying home," smirked his supervisor.

"Well, I can't do that," Stuart replied.

"You better figure something out, Stuart. If you don't, you're not long for this job," his frustrated supervisor stated matter of factly.

Stuart completed his eight-hour shift. He barely paid attention to his work and made the quick swim home one-half foot away. He told Sheryl what his supervisor said. She slammed her tail down on the table, looked at him and yelled, "Well, how are we going to do this?"

"Maybe we should look over our finances," Stuart suggested.

They reviewed their financial portfolio and figured out that Stuart could take eight weeks off, comfortably, without them dipping into their savings.

Then the seahorse couple realized, in unison, that he would quit the plankton factory.

He went in the next day and handed in his resignation.

"But why?" asked Stuart's shocked supervisor. "Is it because we decided you couldn't go home and be daddy to your 2,000 new babies?" she taunted.

"Yes, that's exactly why. I think you and the rest of the 'leaders' in this organization need to get with the times," said Stuart, as he floated out the door, not looking back.

At home, with Sheryl and the 2,000 newborns, was Stuart's happy place. He and Sheryl balanced and shared the duties of raising these 2,000 new needy spirits, keeping them safe from harm's way, and teaching them how to forage for plankton.

Each night, Sheryl and Stuart would talk through the paternity-leave issue when they had a moment alone together.

"There has to be a solution to this," Stuart said. "I know it's an issue around the world, and I know that men everywhere, whether you're a seahorse or human, are always looking for ways to support paternity leave. We must stick together for the sake of women, men, businesses, society, and, most importantly, the children who need time with their mothers and fathers."

Stuart's words sparked an idea in Sheryl's mind. "Stuart, there must be other fathers that have the same issue as you."

"Yes, absolutely," he said. "There were many that were fired."

"Why don't you reach out to all of them and discover if maybe you all can come up with a solution together?" Sheryl suggested.

Stuart called his five colleagues, who were unceremoniously escorted out of the building when they took their paternity leave, and invited them to dinner that night.

He said, "I have something I want to talk to you about."

The six male seahorses floated around eating plankton and discussing paternity leave. After several hours they came up with a solution.

"What if, instead of us trying to fight the system, we created a new one?" said Stuart.

"What do you mean?" asked the seahorses, looking puzzled.

"Well," explained Stuart, "from my experience in customer service, if one seahorse is complaining, hundreds aren't. They're suffering in silence, and I'm sure other seahorses have had issues with paternity leave too."

"Well, yeah," Stuart's five seahorse colleagues nodded in agreement." They each knew a minimum of five male seahorses.

After their meeting, the word spread like wildfire through mangrove trees, roots, sponges, and soft corals.

Within three weeks, Stuart and 300 other seahorses began working together to create a new paternity-leave agency. They would work with employers to assist in finding ways to meet the needs of working fathers and offering them family leave, flexible scheduling, and affordable childcare options.

They consulted with the organizations to shift their mindset around allowing fathers to take full paternity leave and eliminating passive-aggressive language or pressure tactics and break to time with their babies. to discourage fathers from taking their earned break.

Some fathers remained reluctant to take full advantage of this support, despite wanting to be equal partners with their female seahorses in childcare. With all the diapering, meal planning, carpooling, etc., that parenting entails. Family-leave policies and parenting culture in the sea were a point of concern, worry, and embarrassment.

Stuart's company, Fathers Inc., helped thousands of fathers and organizations implement successful paternity leave systems, working not only on the systems but also on the organizations' mindset.

Within one year, they had helped more than 10,000 seahorse fathers successfully take paternity leave. Ironically, the more fathers took paternity leave, the more productive and profitable the organizations became. This was because parenting evolved into a co-creative process with their partners.

His company also eased the pressure on the females being the sole caregivers. The males and females shouldered raising 2,000 babies per family unit. The parenting responsibilities spread more evenly, and both parents were able to rest. Slowly, the culture shifted in the sea, and more seahorses took advantage of the new way to parent. They created workplace cultures that supported paternity leave where all employees benefited, which resulted in happier, healthier, well-adjusted children.

THE END

THE MORAL

Fathers want to be part of their children's lives. Instituting paternity leave has far-reaching benefits.

THREE QUESTIONS

Do you think paternity leave is important? Why or why not?

_____

_____

_____

_____

Can you recognize a time that you participated in a gendered norm/role? Did that make you feel validated? Invalidated? (There is no wrong answer. It is important to recognize and evaluate your own identity, and then consider the perspective of others.)

_____

_____

_____

_____

_____

Do you think gender norms have a place in contemporary society? Why or why not?

_____

_____

_____

_____

III

The Cheetah and the Book of Rest

CHEETAH

Acinonyx jubatus

Once upon a time, Conchita Cheetah was in her prime. She was the fastest big cat in her pride. Conchita could reach up to 70 miles per hour without breaking a sweat. She chose to chase prey at half that speed, right around 35 miles per hour, because it just wasn't fair constantly winning against helpless prey that didn't know any better.

After a chase, Conchita would rest to reset for the next hunt. She was a member of a coalition of cheetahs along with her three older brothers, who fed the pride. She joined the coalition to defend their territory against the other males in the surrounding areas. Female cheetahs are solitary animals, and Conchita was no exception to that rule. Hunting for her was an art; a sense of purpose and, dare she say, pride? Conchita spent most of her life roaming and hunting alone.

The only time that she'd meet up with other cheetahs was to mate. Female cheetahs often raise their cubs for two years; then, the cubs leave to form their own coalition or live alone. Conchita had already had two sets of cubs that she raised. She was done being a mother and now loved to run.

Recently, after her obligatory hunt to find prey for her coalition, her brothers began demanding more food. Honestly, she thought they were bottomless pits and became increasingly irritated. After a chase, she would need a half hour to catch her breath before she ate to fuel her body for the next hunt. Conchita was the top hunter for miles around. This fact was a blessing and a curse. She was a skilled and efficient predator that tried her best to satisfy her brothers' endless need for food. As a result, she stopped taking her half-hour post-hunt respite.

In fact, over the years, her rest period whittled away to 25 minutes, and then 15 minutes, then 10, and then 0. Conchita never realized the physical effects until, one day, she started to feel exhausted and sluggish. Simple tasks that used to bring her joy and pleasure, like grooming herself or purring, were just too overwhelming to attempt. She was constantly stressed out, quick to get angry, and her spots began to fall off her once-shiny coat.

She would snap when her brothers or another female made a simple request. The tipping point came when she came close to biting a cub's head off when it begged for a piece of her meal. Conchita removed herself from her pride to do some soul searching. As she wandered the plains, she thought, "I'm living in an incredibly stressful time, and I feel a little crispy around the edges. I'm physically and emotionally exhausted."

She started to feel her joints ache and her muscles tense. Conchita was seven years old and in the prime of her life, with another seven years ahead of her. Yet the fatigue was so profound and heavy that it felt like it had permeated every fiber of her being while simultaneously suffocating her.

Much to her chagrin, she made an appointment with a cheetah psychiatrist and went in for her first appointment. She did it on a day when her brothers were busy napping in the sun, after an all-night feast on Conchita's latest kill. By scheduling her appointment at this time of day, she knew she could keep her visit to the cheetah psychiatrist a secret. Asking for help was frowned upon in her family. And on top of all the chronic stress, the last thing Conchita needed was judgment.

Conchita arrived at Dr. Katz's office and collapsed into the fluffy couch closest to her but, like the other female cheetahs in her family, she was born restless and didn't sit down for long. She began pacing, feeling nervous, and getting in her head. Conchita didn't notice when Dr. Katz entered the room and said, "Conchita, I'm ready for you now." She snapped out of it, walked in, and sat on Dr. Katz's couch.

Dr. Katz kindly smiled and asked, "What brings you to my office today, Conchita?"

"Well," Conchita said, hesitating and then blurting out, "I'm no longer breathing."

"What do you mean?" said Dr. Katz.

"Well," said Conchita, still hesitant, "after I run and chase prey successfully, I normally, or back in the day, used to take 30 minutes to catch my breath. Now, I don't rest like that anymore."

"Why?" Katz asked.

"I don't have time," Conchita said, getting irritated.

"What do you mean you don't have time?" said Dr. Katz, gently.

Conchita continued, "Because I've become such a prolific hunter. I'm so quick. Not only am I feeding the coalition of my three lazy brothers, but I'm feeding four other coalitions in the area, and that's a lot of work. But I love to run. I just love it. What's happening, doctor, is I'm just feeling exhausted. And I started to get tension headaches. And my sleep patterns are off. I mean, normally, after a good hunt, I can sleep deeply and wake up refreshed, but not anymore. Every time I close my eyes, I feel like there's an electric charge through my body. I can't relax. Sleep deprivation is adding to my stress levels. I just feel like I'm on autopilot."

"Hmm," thought Dr. Katz before saying, "well, I may have something that can help you."

"I'm not taking drugs," snapped Conchita. "So you can put the prescription pad away."

Dr. Katz held up her paw and said, "No, I have a book for you."

She reached behind her on a bookshelf and grabbed a book called *Untamed* by Glennon Doyle.

"Let's start with this book, Conchita. Suspend disbelief, read this book, and we'll talk about it during next week's session," Dr. Katz said, gently.

Conchita snatched the book from Dr. Katz's paw, nodded her head in thanks, and walked out.

Frustrated and shaking, she thought, "A book is what's going to help me?! Well, nothing else has worked. So let me try this."

Under cover of some brush on the plains, Conchita opened the wild-colored book by Glennon Doyle. "Great," she thought sarcastically. "This book starts with a trip to the zoo. I hate zoos. A story about one of my relatives held captive. Wonderful!" A little voice inside her reminded her to suspend disbelief. She continued to read the story about a trip Glennon Doyle took to the zoo with her wife and daughters, describing one exhibit where they saw cheetah Tabitha and her canine companion Mini.

"Oh my god," Conchita gasped. "That's my cousin Tabitha. I always wondered where she ended up. But no one wants to talk about Tabitha's whereabouts."

She continued reading with interest. Glennon Doyle recounted what she saw that day. Mini, the canine companion, is running and catching a stuffed rabbit toy, and Tabitha is doing the same.

"Wait a second. My cousin Tabitha, the fiercest big cat in the country, is now following and mimicking a dog. What in the heck is going on?" Conchita said out loud to no one.

What Doyle saw was a tamed Tabitha whose life was contained within the fencing of her cage, lacking true purpose. Tabitha had lost her wild.

"Oh, my God!" thought Conchita, "I've lost my wild too! The humans trained it out of Tabitha, and now I'm training it out of myself!" Conchita burst into tears as she read Doyle's words.

"You're not crazy. You're a goddamn cheetah. Goddamn right I am!" Conchita thought as she closed the book. Something's got to change. She called to make her second appointment with Dr. Katz.

The next week, Conchita walked into Dr. Katz's office and said, "I know I'm not crazy or hysterical, and I'm a goddamn cheetah. What do I do now?"

Dr. Katz looked at her and asked, "What did you learn from the book?"

"I learned that I'm burnt out. I inadvertently trained myself to be that way and other cheetahs to treat me that way."

"Say more," nudged Dr. Katz.

"Well," Conchita continued, "I believed in the narrative that the other cheetahs were telling me. I believed that to have value, I had to give them more and more and more. I had to do it faster than any other cheetah, continue working harder, and neglect my own needs. I fell into that trap that external forces created for me."

"Good awareness," Dr. Katz encouraged. "What are you gonna do about it?"

"Well, I'm going to revive my exercise routine. I love doing morning yoga, and 'cat-cow' is my favorite pose, allowing me to quiet my mind and flow," Conchita said.

Dr. Katz nodded in agreement, "Gentle stretching and deep breathing provide an abundance of health benefits, including healing your burnout. Regardless of how much energy you may have on a given day, if you can get some sort of physical exercise or meditation, that will always be a helpful coping tool. And, Conchita, physical exercise doesn't mean hunting."

Conchita nodded her head in understanding.

Katz continued, "The other thing I'd love to have you add, Conchita, is mindfulness. You enter a state of a relaxed body and calm, observant mind. You observe your external environment but don't engage with it, and you witness how your mind reacts to the stimuli."

"Mindfulness," repeated Conchita.

"Mindfulness," Dr. Katz explained, "revolves around trying to be as emotionally present as possible. One way to do this is deep breathing.

Every time you capture and kill prey, I want you to sit there and deeply breathe. Breathe in for a count of three. Hold your breath for a count of three. And slowly exhale audibly for a count of eight. In doing that, you're focused on the moment. You're present. It's easy to do and doesn't require any equipment."

Dr. Katz added with a wink, "It doesn't require drugs. No other cheetah will know that you're doing deep breathing, and they'll just think you're catching your breath after a kill."

Conchita enthusiastically nodded, adding to Dr. Katz's plan for her, "I want to make sure that I set good work-life boundaries because I feel like the lines between my brothers and me and the other coalitions of cheetahs have blurred. I can't tell the difference between when I'm hunting and living my life."

"It's important," Dr. Katz added, "to say, 'Okay, I've put in a hard day's work. Now I need to press stop and attend to social aspects of my life, things that are just fun and relaxing.'"

"I love the idea of that," said Conchita. "It's been a long time since I took time to groom myself and just lay on my back in the sun. It's time to enforce work-life boundaries. And I'd love to go back to my hobby of finding small, unknown watering holes every three days and just laying around and looking at my reflection. That's one of my favorite hobbies."

"Then that's what you need to do," Dr. Katz agreed with Conchita's plan, "Because you don't want to be known as 'Conchita the burnt-out cheetah.'"

"No, I don't," Conchita thought aloud. "I can't continue this way, because I'm going to die an early death, and I want to enjoy the last seven years of my life."

Conchita went home and began practicing all these things, immediately seeing results. She could relax and cut down on the number of coalitions she hunted for, hunting only for her brothers, which enabled her to resume her post-hunt rests. Conchita fell in love, again spotting prey five kilometers away with her fantastic eyesight. She rekindled her passion for hunting during the day, while relaxing at night. Eventually, the aches disappeared, her spots returned, and her coat shone. The fatigue left her body, and the tension headaches disappeared. Conchita redesigned her life, living it with mindfulness, intention, joy, and happiness.

THE END

THE MORAL

Burnout has become an epidemic. The American Institute of Stress found that 75% of all doctors visits are stress-related. Burnout can have serious consequences for both employees and employers. According to a study by the Harvard Business Review, burnout costs American businesses $300 billion per year.

THREE QUESTIONS

Can you recognize a time you felt that too much was being asked of you? (Whether it's a family member, a teacher, a boss, or a friend, everyone has had this feeling. It is important to recognize that, working with it to better advocate for yourself in the future.)

_____

_____

_____

_____

How can you advocate for yourself the next time someone asks something that is too much for you to handle?

_____

_____

_____

_____

What do you like to do to relax and care for yourself? How can you incorporate more of this into your everyday life?

_____

_____

_____

_____

The Hippo, the Rhino,
and the Elephant

HIPPO, RHINO, ELEPHANT

Hippopotamus amphibious, Rhinocerotidae, Elephantidae

Once upon a time, at a place in the desert where all the animals would gather and affectionately call it the cooler water spot, a rhino and hippo conversed.

"Yeah, I repaired my horn. I sure did," the rhino showed off his horn proudly.

The hippo said, "Wow, it looks good. And I can't even tell you were in a fight with a poacher; you'd never know. I only knew it because I saw it with my own eyes! It was an epic battle."

"The poacher fight followed the fight with the elephants. Yeah, these new horn-growing supplements have made my horn stronger and bigger."

Down the lane from the water cooler stood a herd of elephants. The elephants couldn't help but overhear the conversation, catching only bits and pieces and not knowing the context. They concluded through assumptions that the rhino was extremely horny.

The elephants, chuckling to themselves, thought the story was so funny it had to be shared. Of course, they would be discreet and whisper it down the lane. The first group the elephants came upon were the hyenas; they relayed the story of the horny rhino, and the pack of hyenas fell over in a fit of laughter.

"A horny rhino! That's a great story! Oh, my goodness, wait until we tell the flock of hornbills. They're going to love this!" the hyenas squealed with laughter.

The story of the horny rhino spread like wildfire burning hot and quick like gossip often does; this went on for days and days until everybody in the Sahara Desert was talking about this horny, oversexed rhino.

"...Did you hear?" "I mean, I'm not surprised." "Rhinos are crazy." "They love sex, so it makes sense." The rumors swirled throughout the animal kingdom, but no one thought to speak directly to the rhino to check the story's validity.

When the gossip landed at the rhino's doorstep, as rumors often do, he was distraught. He had worked hard to use all his natural resources plus some supplements to regrow his horn after defending his clash with death from persistent predators.

Plus, there were poachers in the area—the night after his fight with the elephants, he got caught in a poacher trap. The humans descended on him, trying to cut off his horn. Luckily, their knives broke. The rhino was able to break free from the trap and escape.

Regrowing his horn had an almost spiritual significance to him, a re-birth, if you will. To have his transformation story twisted into fodder for a bunch of gossips made him sick to his stomach. The narrative cast him as a sexual deviant, and he was pissed.

The rhino decided to do the only thing he could do; the only thing in his power. He went to find the source of the rumor. He knew who it was, but he just had to confirm a few things. It wasn't hard to do that. He talked to the hyenas, and they're always willing to spill the beans.

He approached the pack of hyenas and took the direct approach.

"Have you heard a rumor about me?" He asked.

They fell over and giggled, unable to control their laughter. Finally, the hyenas blurted out in unison, "You mean the rumor that you're a sex-crazed deviant who's so horny that you cannot go without sex for an hour? Yeah, we've heard that; everyone's telling that story, and we've heard that from several different animals."

The rhino suppressed anger rising inside of his body. "Well, do you know where the rumor started?" he asked.

"We heard that there was a herd of elephants that overheard the conversation between you and the hippo, so that it might be one of them."

"Elephants? Why do I always have to address the elephant in the room?" the rhino thought, shaking his head.

"Thanks," said the rhino, walking away. As he got further away from the hyenas, the rhino heard peals of laughter erupt.

He felt heat rushing to the surface of his skin. "Isn't that the worst feeling when you walk away and somebody starts laughing? And you know it's them talking about you? Well, I'm going to get to the bottom of this."

He mustered up all his courage, and went to where the herd of elephants stood. There was a female elephant that he knew well. He stomped over to her and asked, "Hey, how are you doing? What's going on?"

She gave him the side-eye and was hesitant to talk to him. She couldn't decide if it was because he startled her by coming up from behind.

"Things are good," she said, giving him the benefit of the doubt.

The rhino continued, "I'm upset."

"Really. Why?" the elephant asked, feigning ignorance.

"Well," he explained. "There's a rumor about me, and I want to get to the bottom of it, and I need to find the source. Will you help?"

The elephant flirtatiously gazed at the rhino before asking, "Any truth to this rumor?" A hopeful tone in her voice.

"What? That I'm horny? No! I just regrew my horn after two fights!" he yelled.

But, like a game of telephone, gossip often leaves out the truth's context, nuances, and facts. The real story no longer existed in its original form. The rhino continued, "This rumormonger has said I have sexual escapades."

"Really?" The elephant said, sounding disappointed. "I know who said that. It was the head elephant. The one you fought off your turf. I'm not getting in the middle of this, and you'll have to talk to him yourself."

"Oh, I plan to address it directly. Thanks," said the rhino.

He marched up to the head elephant and addressed him, alpha male to alpha male. He stood about 500 yards from the cooler water spot surrounded by his herd.

"Hey! You!" shouted the rhino. "I need a word with you in private."

The head elephant turned his head, while tossing that dirt on his back to keep himself cool and responded, "come on over." His herd dispersed, staying within earshot and just close enough to come to their leader's rescue in case things turned ugly.

The rhino thought it was ironic that he was throwing dirt on his back because all the head elephant did was sling mud at him.

When the rhino and the head elephant finally stood toe to toe, the rhino stated, "I hear you've spread some gossip. Saying that I'm horny."

The head elephant said, "Yeah, I'll never forget it because I heard you tell the hippo that you were horny."

"No, that's not what I was telling the hippo," said the rhino angrily. "The hippo was there the night after you and I fought for territory, and I won."

The rhino had to get in a jab or two.

He continued, "Then I escaped from a poacher's trap and dodged their knives. Not before they could land a few strikes on my face with their machetes. My horn was hanging half off my face. That hippo, who happens to be my friend, was giving me advice on how to grow it back naturally. And all the advice he gave me worked. What you overhead was me showing him my horn and thanking him for his help. After all the pain, struggle, and hard work of healing, you made up something that wasn't true about me; I'm hurt. Why would you do that? And why wouldn't you come to me directly?"

The elephant looked at him and said, "Because I thought it was a funny story that would entertain the animal kingdom."

"Well, it wasn't your story to tell, it was mine. And you didn't even get the story right. You don't even have the facts or the proper context. And now it's hurt my reputation around the cooler water spot. Do you know that gossip makes it challenging to experience honest, meaningful relationships? Do you know that it puts us in a negative critical mood? Do you know it's a waste of time? It is such a terrible way to communicate."

The elephant looked at him, and, in a split second, he realized that the rhino was right. He realized that instead of talking about the rhino, he could have spoken to the rhino, and he missed out on a great opportunity.

The elephant looked at him and sincerely said, "I'm so sorry. You're right. I apologize for my thoughtlessness and didn't mean to hurt you. What can I do to make it right?"

"You make it right by apologizing, and that takes courage and humility. Thank you for asking what you could do differently. There's a magic phrase that I say when animals come and start to tell me gossip; I ask them, 'Why they are telling me this?' Maybe you could try that in the future," the rhino said.

"That's a great tip," said the elephant.

"And the other thing you can do is just not gossip," the rhino continued.

"If you haven't seen it firsthand or heard it directly from the source, you shouldn't believe it. And if someone honors you with the trust of telling you the true story, it's not your story to tell."

The elephant sighed, "You're so right. Gossip does hurt. I'm going to stop it right now. Thank you for addressing the elephant in the room, Mr. Rhino," the elephant said.

"You're welcome," said the rhino. "Please stop talking about me."

"I will," the elephant assured him.

From that day forward, any time an animal would come up and try to gossip with the elephant about anyone, he would stop them and say, "I don't gossip because it's not fair to the animal you're talking about" Then he would walk away.

THE END

THE MORAL

Gossip can damage lives.
Some negative consequences of workplace gossip are:

- *Erosion of trust and morale.*
- *Lost productivity and wasted time.*
- *Increased anxiety among employees, as rumors circulate without clear information as to what is and isn't fact.*
- *Divisiveness among employees as people take sides.*
- *Hurt feelings and reputations.*
- *Attrition due to good employees leaving the company because of an unhealthy work environment.*

THREE QUESTIONS

Can you recognize a time that you participated in gossip? If so, what was it about? (Everyone, at one point or another, participates in gossip. It is important to recognize that and to work toward overcoming it.)

_____

_____

_____

_____

What are the negative effects of gossip?

_____

_____

_____

How can you approach gossip when it comes up in your everyday life?

_____

_____

_____

_____

The Prestigious Stray

DOMESTIC SHORTHAIR CAT
Felis cactus

Once upon a time, a male tabby cat was born in a land known as the City of Brotherly Love and Sisterly Affection, aka Philadelphia, Pennsylvania. The conditions of his birth were unusual. His mother got knocked up by a local tomcat. She gave birth to her litters in an abandoned row house in West Philly.

The first days of his life were tough. He was born in darkness. He had twelve brothers and sisters, and they all fought each other hard for food to eat. Finally, when he was six months old, he had had it. This green-eyed, pink-nosed kitten had had it—living in a boarded up, smelly, moldy old row house that never had any affection or light was not the life he dreamed of. He was meant for bigger and better things. The kitten decided to take control of his life and escape.

He found a small opening that the sun shone through. He peeked out and noticed it was the second story.

"Well, anyone can do easy," thought the kitten. He closed his eyes, leaped into the sunlight, and landed on the ground in the back alley that ran behind the houses. It was early in the morning, and he could hear the birds whistling in the trees. The kitten stopped for a moment, lifted his nose, and inhaled the fresh air. It was nice not to have to push his siblings out of the way to give himself some space.

Walking down the road, he saw a woman in her pajamas with two dogs in the back of one of the neighboring houses. He didn't understand this type of animal. He did know one thing for sure, where there are humans, there is food.

The dogs looked happy, healthy, and calm. They, unlike him, didn't look hungry. His stomach was always growling, and his ribs were sticking out. He figured he'd walk up to the woman; what's the worst that could happen? She shoos him away. So, what?

He casually strolled over to where she was standing and rubbed himself on her legs. Then looked up with his large kitten eyes. The woman startled at first and then softened immediately when their eyes met.

She leaned down and gently stroked his head. He pressed his face into her hand. The kitten had never felt such a soft, gentle touch. Even after he was born, the only time his mother touched him was to groom his coat roughly. Once she was done, she'd cast him off like garbage.

The woman bent to pick him up, saying, "Let me see who you belong to. A friendly little fellow like you must have a collar. Wow! I guess not," she said.

Realizing he had no collar and no home to speak of, she lifted him to her chest; the feeling of her arms around him made him feel safe. He heard her heartbeat and snuggled down, positioning himself above her heart. He lost himself in the gentle rhythm and began to purr a full-body purr. The woman was enjoying this peaceful moment with the kitten as well.

"No, no, no, no!" snapping out of her early-morning reverie. "We can't have a cat. I'm allergic, and we already have two dogs. We can't have a cat!" She gently placed him on the ground and took the dogs inside the house.

The kitten thought "I would've liked to live with them, and she seemed nice." As he began to walk away, the woman returned with a man in PJs. They left the dogs inside the house, and the man picked him up. The same feeling the woman gave the little kitten returned in the man's arms. The kitten felt so safe, he began to knead his paws on the man's face.

He looked at the woman with a twinkle and said, "Friendly little fellow, isn't he? I call this (referring to the kitten's paws on his face), 'puffing pillows.'"

The woman smiled at the love her husband was pouring into a little stray cat he'd just met. Her husband continued, "I guess, Kelly, we have ourselves a cat."

"Yes, Brian," Kelly said. "I guess we do."

They opened the basement door, and the cat boldly walked between the two dogs that had been living in this house for much longer. But he didn't care, and he had courage and swagger.

"Wow!" giggled Kelly. "He acts like a boss. Strutting in here like he owns the place! Let's name him Pablo Escobar."

Brian agreed, "Welcome home, Pablo Escobar, or should I say, 'Hola Pablito?'"

Pablo lived a happy life with a couple and their two dogs. Dogs raised him. Kelly and Brian often found Pablo laying across the front paws of their dogs and grooming their heads as they rested on the floor.

Pablo was well-fed and well-cared for by all members of the household. He wanted to contribute to the family the only way he knew how, mouse control. Pablo was so skilled that Brian often exclaimed, "Well, we picked the right name for him. He is the deadliest cat in town."

As Pablo grew older, he yearned to do more with his life, but all he really wanted to do was catch mice. He applied for job after job and got rejected each time. Until finally, one day, he decided to create his own business, Nite Nite Mice. Restaurant owners in his area began to hire him to clean up their mouse problem. Pablo would go into the businesses at night and take care of all the mice before dawn. His calling card was always, "Nite, Nite Mice," a sign of respect for the deceased and a signal of a completed job well done.

Word of Pablo's business spread quietly among the restaurant community, and nobody wanted anyone to know that they had mice in their establishments. Nite, Nite Mice became so good at coming and going undetected that their services required more and more cats. Pablo only hired cats from historically underrepresented communities or kill shelters.

Suddenly, all the big mouse control companies lost big contracts to Pablo Escobar's company, filled with misfits, rebels, rejects, and death row cats. He began to get calls from these companies for meetings, trying to figure out why Pablo's "little" company was eating into their market share.

Pablo's company was so successful that the oldest, most prominent, and wealthiest mouse control company, PCO (Pedigreed Cats Only), Ltd. est. in 1682, called a meeting of its board of directors, and it was decided that they'd either convince Pablo to work for them or they'd acquire "Nite, Nite Mice."

They knew they couldn't get Pablo to work for them, because he'd turned down their offers many times. Then they made him an offer that was too good to pass up, at least without a conversation.

Pablo found himself in a meeting about acquiring his company. He walked into a big dark-paneled conference room. There sat 12 long-haired show cats. Their coats were long and snowy white, and not one hair was out of place. Their eyes were crystal blue, as if they could peer into your soul.

He was greeted by the cat seated at the head of the table in a very direct unemotional tone, "Sit down Mr. Escobar, please make yourself comfortable. My name is Griffin Hemingway Johnson V. You can call me Griff."

Pablo looked around and thought he was hallucinating because every cat looked the same and sounded the same. "They did say make myself comfortable," he thought. He chose the seat at the other end of the table across from Griff. Once seated, he stretched out his back leg and began to groom himself.

A hush fell over the room and one of the show cats let out an audible gasp. "What are you doing," Griff said disgusted.

"You told me to make myself comfortable. That's what I was doing. When I'm comfortable, I groom myself," said Pablo. "Usually, I let the dogs who raised me do the work for me."

"Wait! You were raised by dogs?! You groom yourself?! Pablo, we must tell you, pedigree and proper behavior is very important to us. None of the cats seated around this table groom themselves. Our blood is as blue as our eyes. Our ancestors came over on the Mayflower," Griff continued. "When it's time for our daily grooming, our humans do that for us. We have a one-hour session every morning where they brush and clean us."

Pablo, not impressed, said, "And how's that working out for you, Griff?"

"Well, look at us. We all come from the same line. We all come from the same relatives of show families," stated Griff proudly.

"Well, that explains why there is no diversity in any one of you. It also explains to me why you need me more than I need you," Pablo responded.

Griff threw his head back and laughed. "Oh, Pablo. You're so funny." Which was a passive-aggressive way of putting him down.

Pablo was not going to take the bait. He knew his worth. "My intention was not to be funny at all. I'm just commenting on observable fact."

"And what's that?" asked Griff.

"You all look the same. You all sound the same and your business is failing. Because you're all taking the same approach with the same unconscious biases, which is why I'm taking the majority of your business."

Griff's tone changed immediately, narrowing his blue eyes at Pablo, "Ah, yes. How are you doing that?"

Pablo met Griff's gaze and said, "By being the fastest, deadliest, most-trained tabby cat in all of Philadelphia and having a group of diverse cats who know how to get the job done in innovative and creative ways."

Pablo had contracts all over the city. Mouse hunting was in his blood. He found out recently through a DNA test that he was connected or related distantly Pablo Purrcaso, the cat that discovered the famous mouse Midas, the mouse artist in the Metropolitan Museum of Art.

Pablo let the show cats talk their talk—their highbrow, egotistical talk that veiled their insults and insecurity. Every time they asked him what it would cost to buy his company, he'd stop grooming himself and calmly say, "you don't have enough money." He knew power, position, and privilege meant nothing when it came to killing mice. He kept calm and kept grooming himself which seemed to irritate the members of PCO, Ltd. even more.

"How do you know that?" Griff asked.

"I just know, and word on the street has confirmed my suspicions. Plus, I always do my due diligence before coming to a meeting like this; our forensic accountant found out some interesting things about your books. I have to tell you, you need to think outside the litter box if you think your business is going to survive, because based on my numbers," Pablo pulled out the file of research he compiled on PCO, Ltd. before continuing.

"Nite, Nite Mice has taken 30% of your business in just half a year. By the end of the year, we project we'll secure 50% of your market share. With my diverse team, our innovative efforts, and stellar reputation, you need me more than I need you. So, let's stop the posturing and let's make a deal, shall we?"

The haggling went back and forth for hours. There was a catfight at one point. One of the executive assistants had to come in and separate all of them.

Finally, they came to an agreement. Pablo would take over the CEO position, retain creative control, the name of the company, and hiring decisions. He'd oversee a multi-billion-dollar, mouse-control corporation.

After they inked the deal, Pablo became boss and the city of Philadelphia's restaurant community was rid of mice. PCO, Ltd rebranded to Nite, Nite Mice, and became the largest global mouse control company in the world, with the most diverse workers in their industry vertical. Diversity and inclusion was a moral imperative for everyone who worked with Pablo and his leadership team. The organization reaped the benefits by expanding their customer base and their revenue streams. Their diverse team members drove conversations that led to expansion of products and services to address segments of the market that were ignored or missed by PCO, Ltd.

They also cut the amount of show cats on the board from 12 to 2, making sure that all different kinds of cats from different backgrounds were included—and they even recruited two mixed-breed dogs. The company continued to thrive for generations.

THE END

THE MORAL

Taking a holistic approach to diversity, equity, inclusion, and accessibility can drive revenue, innovation, and growth, creating a psychologically safe space for people to thrive at work.

THREE QUESTIONS

Can you recognize a bias that you have? If so, what is it? (Everyone has some kind of bias in them. It is important to recognize that and to work toward overcoming it.)

_____

_____

_____

_____

_____

What is one thing that you could do to actively learn from someone of a different background/perspective than your own?

_____

_____

_____

_____

_____

How can you be an advocate for diversity, equity, and inclusion?

_____

_____

_____

_____

_____

VI

The Righteous Black Tourmaline Horn

UNICORN

Legendary Mystical creature

Once upon a time, there was a beautiful little unicorn filly named Aurora. When this magical creature was born, she was wrapped in love and light.

In fact, when the baby unicorn drew her first breath, the skies were lit up with the most amazing colors of sun beams, painting light-filled canvas the likes of which no one had ever seen before that moment in time.

Her parents gave her the name Aurora. Aurora is a mystical and romantic name that means "dawn" in Latin. An aurora also refers to a natural light display in the Earth's sky called the aurora polaris, or polar lights, visible only in high-latitude regions like the North and South Poles. The Aurora Borealis (the Northern Lights) and the Aurora Australis (the Southern Lights) paint the sky in a dazzling array of colors.

Aurora was the Roman goddess of the dawn. Helios, the sun god, and Selene, the moon goddess, were her brother and sister. Aurora rode across the sky each morning before her brother Helios rode across with the sun. As she rode, she sprinkled dew over the land.

And everywhere Aurora the unicorn went, she brought light. She brought fun. She bought love. She brought her healing powers.

Aurora loved to adorn herself. She tied all kinds of crystals into her curly black mane, put feathers in her tail, and added glitter to her coat. Aurora was unique in every sense of the word.

Instead of having a horn made of gold, her horn was made of black tourmaline. Every time somebody would come near her with bad energy, she would simply wave her horn in the air, transforming the negative feelings into good new energy.

She loved to play and loved putting out good energy into the world.

As she grew older, the other unicorns became less receptive to her energy. As she entered the workforce into the corporate stall space, she got great evaluations from her bosses, except for one thing that was constantly brought up.

It always started the same way, "Aurora, you're wonderful, but your mane and your tail are unruly, and your black tourmaline horn is very distracting. We recommend you straighten your hair and tail and dye your horn gold."

Aurora thought this is what she had to do in order to be successful. She spent hundreds of thousands of dollars and a lot of her "free" time dyeing her horn gold and straightening her mane, so that she could fit in. Aurora wanted to belong so badly.

Every time she did, though, she felt a little piece of her die inside. In fact, a tiny piece of her horn would chip off every time she applied the gold dye. She became irritable and fatigue took up space in her bones.

"I don't understand why I can't just be myself. When I was younger, every space I came into was made better by my horn and my energy," she thought to herself.

Little by little, her horn started to shrink, falling off her head piece by piece. This forced conformity chipped away at Aurora until she was unrecognizable even to herself.

She tried to shapeshift herself into what she thought others around her wanted and what they thought success looked like for her. Each time she endured the laborious task of straightening her mane and tail, followed by dyeing her horn, Aurora became more and more angry.

One day she caught her reflection in a mirror hanging in the hallway of the corporate stalls. She had to look twice because she didn't recognize herself. Aurora couldn't take it anymore. "I don't need this," she thought to herself. "I'm beautiful and magical just the way I am. I'm not spending more time or money to sacrifice pieces of my horn and soul for this job. I quit."

She left her corporate job. With a friend, she started a business focusing on educating corporate stall companies on how to make space for every creature just as they are.

Due to all the trauma she experienced in the corporate stall world changing her appearance, being told not to act like a victim, having her words manipulated and then used against her, and having her ideas stolen, she started seeing a therapist because people kept asking her why she was so angry. She had been labeled "the angry unicorn," and she couldn't understand why people wanted her to change her when, in her natural state, she exuded magic.

Her therapist, a kind, older doctor unicorn named Hippocrates, shared a valuable piece of wisdom with Aurora during one of her first sessions after she told him she was tired of being labeled "angry."

"Aurora, you know, there are three things underneath anger, right?"

Aurora shook her head, "no."

"The three things below anger are: 1) hurt feelings, 2) a blow to self-esteem or 3) a blow to self-image."

"Well, doc, I have all three. I don't understand why people expect me to change," said Aurora sadly.

"Even if you feel someone is pressuring you to change, you still have a choice. The power is always in the decisions you make for yourself. It sounds to me like your workplace is filled with toxic leaders."

Aurora agreed with her doctor's assessment. She pondered his words during her walk home.

She knew her value was in the unique gifts and talents she brought the world. Aurora decided then and there, she would no longer straighten her mane and tail or dye her black tourmaline horn gold.

As soon as she made that decision, she felt the light swell inside her, and something shifted.

Aurora began to take baby steps back towards her authentic self, and her magic grew. She became more powerful and energized, and began to heal every space that she came into. In fact, anybody who was around her at this moment in time was bathed in her beautiful energy. The light that was once smothered by fatigue and frustration spilled back into their bodies and became happier again through that energetic transfer.

It was a joy to be around Aurora.

"Well," Aurora thought, "I am named after the Goddess of Light. And since I stopped changing myself for others, stepped into my healing power, and asked to be surrounded by my angels and ancestors, I became more myself. I was able to leverage more of myself to help others."

THE END

THE MORAL

Trying to make people conform removes their unique magical essence.

THREE QUESTIONS

Can you recognize a time that you judged someone for not conforming? If so, what was it about? (Everyone has had some kind of judgment about someone who goes against their perspective of normal. It is important to recognize that and to work toward overcoming it.)

_____

_____

_____

_____

_____

_____

What is one word that comes up when you think about conformity?

_____

Do you think that conformity has a role to play in contemporary society? Why or why not?

_____

_____

_____

_____

_____

_____

VII

The Cavalier and the Stranger

CAVALIER KING CHARLES SPANIEL
Canis lupus familiarise

Once upon a time there was a Cavalier King Charles Spaniel named Tessie. She had a red coat and big brown eyes that you could get lost in. Her sweet playful spirit endeared her to everyone she met.

Tessie loved to eat. She loved to play. She was very vocal, often grunting or communicating her needs to her owners through snorts, stomping her feet, or spinning around in a circle. When she slept, Tessie's snoring was so loud and raucous it often concerned her owners because it sounded like she had sleep apnea.

She was a happy dog who was devoted to her owners, often snuggling on their laps or laying on their chests while they meditated. Her mere presence brought joy to any space she occupied. People loved Tess.

In fact, one time, her owners brought her to the dog park and she ran up to a stranger. A man. When Tess' mom went over to retrieve her, the man said, "I'll give you $10,000 for her right now."

Her mother, a woman named Kelly, looked directly at the man and said, "No."

The man persisted, "How much do you want for her?"

Kelly replied, "You cannot afford it and she's not for sale."

"Everything's for sale, name your price," pressured the man. "I looked into her brown eyes and I fell in love."

"Well, that's nice for you but she's our dog, and you'll have to look elsewhere."

"How about my vintage gold rolex?" The man started taking his watch off his wrist.

"What part of no don't you understand, sir?" Kelly asserted.

"I have a vault full of gold you can have, just down the street. We can go now, if you want."

"No," Kelly repeated firmly, not breaking her gaze with the man.

"Wait, I know," said the man, "I have 40 acres down the street in Gladwynne. I'll transfer the deed to you right now. I just need to call my attorney."

"No," said Kelly again, reminding herself that "no" was a complete sentence.

"Come on!" whined the man, "I really want her."

Kelly picked Tess up in her arms, looked directly at the man and said firmly, "We don't always get what we want and money doesn't buy everything." With that she walked away snuggling Tess in her arms. Kelly whispered to Tess, "I love you Tess. Your home is with us."

As Kelly and Tess approached Brian, Kelly's husband he gave her a questioning look, "What was that about?"

Kelly rolled her eyes, "Just another man with power, position, and privilege thinking he can buy anything he wants, including our dog."

Brian shook his head, "No chance in hell," he said picking up Tess. "You're a crucial part of our family.""

THE END

THE MORAL

Money can't buy everything.

THREE QUESTIONS

What's something money can't buy?

_____

_____

_____

_____

What's a money-related stress that comes with having more money?

_____

_____

_____

_____

Is the phrase "money can't buy happiness" true? Why or why not?

_____

_____

_____

_____

VIII

The Golden Agreement

GOLDEN RETRIEVER

Canis lupus familiarise

Once upon a time, there was a Golden Retriever named Karly Love. She was sweet, smart, and beautiful. Karly believed every human she met was her best friend. Everyone loved Karly. And Karly loved everyone.

There was one behavior that Karly wouldn't stop and, try as they might, her owners could not get her to stop. They'd tried everything from blocking her to hiring expensive trainers. Karly just loved to sniff people's crotches.

This became a problem when people would come to her family's house and weren't comfortable with dogs. Before her owners could greet their guests, Karly's had her nose in their crotches.

In fact, it got so bad that her owners' friends started calling her "No Consent Karly."

Consent is an ongoing process of discussing boundaries and what individuals are comfortable with.

Karly wasn't asking for consent nor was she respecting people's boundaries.

Her behavior drove people away or they would refuse to come to the house. No one wants their crotch sniffed. It was a violation of personal space. Karly's behavior made her owners and their guests feel awkward. Honestly, it was borderline assault. As soon as people crossed the threshold of her house, she went headfirst into their crotch.

Karly's owners knew that this behavior could lead to their house guests taking legal action against the owners. And it could potentially lead to them losing Karly. They wanted people to feel relaxed, welcomed, and like they belonged when visiting their home. Karly's owners had to change her behavior immediately before the worst possible scenario happened.

Her owners began to work with Karly daily. They trained and trained and trained, reinforcing what was okay.

They even invited visitors to their house to assist them. When guests entered their home, they were asked to ignore Karly until she settled down. If she approached them, they were asked to turn their bodies away from her. They were instructed not to touch her when she approached them. Karly was only allowed to approach her family's guests if they called her over by name.

They clearly and freely communicated. Her owners and their guests would say, "No, Karly. Go lay down," when her behavior crossed a boundary or violated consent.

Finally, it got to the point that Karly knew what behavior was okay and what required consent because the boundaries were set in place.

Now, when guests come over and they ask Karly to approach them, she sits quietly at their feet, puts one paw on their knee, and, if they say it's okay, puts her head in their lap and gets a scratch around her ears. And when they're done, they tell her to lay down and she lays down. She's no longer "No Consent Karly." She's a sweet golden retriever whose company is enjoyed by all.

THE END

THE MORAL

Consent is an agreement between participants to engage in sexual activity. Consent should be clearly and freely communicated. A verbal and affirmative expression of consent can help both you and your partner to understand and respect each other's boundaries.

THREE QUESTIONS

What is consent?

_____

_____

_____

_____

What's the difference between verbal and written consent?

_____

_____

_____

_____

What situations require written consent?

_____

_____

_____

_____

_____

Midas the Mouse

MOUSE
Mus musculus

Once upon a time, in a land called New York, New York, inside a building called The Metropolitan Museum of Art, lived the 65-millionth generation of mice. The family, known as a mischief of mice, named the Brie family, after the cheese, because for 65 million generations, this family had lived inside the walls of the Metropolitan Museum of Art, and they were the chief cheese chasers. They lived in the walls of the museum because nearly every nook and cranny of the building was within a few meters of food.

Now, what is a cheese chaser, you may ask? Basically, since, April 13, 1870, the Brie family had perfected a route in the Met where special events were occurring. They would then study the meals that were laid out for the humans that occupied this space and would focus on the cheese-heavy events. They loved all kinds of cheese from gruyere to cheddar to your basic American cheese products. The Brie family had dined on a rare cheese produced in Serbia from a breed of rare Balkan donkeys in the Michael C. Rockefeller Wing. They munched on feta in the Greek and Roman Art Gallery. And almost bathed themselves in raclette, which is a type of cheese traditionally used as a melt-over-various-delicious-foods topping that sometimes seems to put fondue to shame.

Really any kind of cheese would do. And because they were a huge family of 50, they had a lot of mouths to feed.

Now, Mr. Brie, the patriarch of the family, was 151th generation cheese chaser at The Met, and he had perfected his skill set of grabbing cheese from these special events and leaving the scene undetected. He brought it back to his family to feed them and stored the rest underneath the air conditioning unit in the utility room in which they lived.

Their youngest son, Midas, was in training to take over the family. He was the only boy of the family, and it was his job to be the next cheese chaser and continue the traditions of the Brie family. Every day, Mr. Brie and Midas would wake up, go over the map of the Metropolitan Museum of Art, and identify the special occasions or special events that were happening that day.

"Good morning, Midas, are you ready for a great cheese chasing day?" said, Mr. Brie cheerily.

Midas, rubbing the sleep out of his eyes, wishing he could rest sighed, "yes, father, I'm ready. I am ready for the day of cheese chasing."

What Midas's father didn't know was Midas had spent all night recreating Van Gogh's *Wheat Fields with Cypresses*. He just couldn't seem to get the movement right. When Midas looked at Van Gogh's work of art, he was transported. He could feel the breeze on his face and hear the cypresses and the wheat dancing in time with the airflow. It was a permanent part of The Met collection. You see, for years after the family was fast asleep, Midas would get up, take his easel and paints out into the museum, and recreate, in miniature-mouse size, the masterpieces that called the building their home.

Midas loved the different types of art that he was exposed to, and he loved combining paints in different textures and techniques to make these masterpieces come alive. He got lost. He would lose hours of time just relaxing and creating with his hands. This was what he was born to do. It was what he was called to do, but he couldn't share the secret with his family because his father, Mr. Brie, was adamant that Midas carry on the traditions of the Brie family, which were now in their almost 152nd generation.

So every morning when Mr. Brie would cheerly wake up Midas, encouraging him to go over the maps and the passageways, so they could move undetected within the walls of this storied museum, Midas would swallow his pride and do his best to honor his father's wishes. Although he went through the motions, his heart was never in it. There were times when Midas would make careless mistakes because his mind would wander off their practiced routes and gaze at the wonderful art that was in the building.

In fact, he almost got caught one time between the sharp claws of the docent's cat, while gazing at the visiting Mona Lisa. He got so lost in it. Why? "What is this woman smirking about?" he wondered to himself. Midas was so deep in thought that he didn't realize that Pablo Purrcasso was creeping up behind him and stalking Midas as his next mouse meal.

Pablo came within an inch of Midas when his father wasn't looking. With experience and quick thinking, Mr. Brie was able to create a distraction to save Midas from the snapping jaws of the museum cat. Mr. Brie realized that he had to sit his son down and explain to him the dangers of the outside world.

"Midas," he said, "I love your sense of adventure AND your appreciation for great art, but you must be more careful. The rules that have been set in place by 65 million generations of our family are there to protect you. That's why we spend so much time planning—to avoid situations like this. I love you, son, but you just have to be more aware and realize that this is not about you. It's about the survival of our family. Family before all."

Midas found himself parroting back exactly what his father wanted to hear. "Yes, father, I understand. I want to be the best cheese chaser in the world." But even as the hollow words were coming out of his mouth, Midas knew they weren't true. In fact, he felt like he was choking back vomit. The idea of being the chief cheese chaser for the family for the rest of his life made him queasy.

A life of hoarding and storing different kind of cheeses so that his family could survive was the last thing he wanted to do with his life. All he wanted to do was get lost in the paints, clay, fashion, and the art that was surrounding them in this beautiful and historic building. He wanted to live a life filled with color, a life of his choosing, a life where he was inspired, a life where he was uplifted, a life where he could create something that would evoke a deep emotional connection that would change the world forever, change the way people saw things, change the way people relate to art and to mice in general.

Every time they got caught chasing cheese, it was, "You're vermin. You're no good. You're worthless garbage." Or it could get even worse, somebody could die. And Midas just did not want to have a life like that, but he also didn't want to disappoint his father. His father was his everything. He loved him dearly and he knew he only had good intentions, but it just was not the life that Midas wanted.

And why? Why? His family had been doing this for generations, and thousands of them had died in the effort. Midas didn't want to lay down his life just to chase cheese. He wanted to create art that would reflect and impact society, but he had no way to tell his father. He couldn't figure it out.

He tried to broach the subject so many times, but anytime he got close to saying, "This is not what I want with my life," his father would say, "You know, your great-great-great grandfather lived in these walls. And he was the one who started this whole cheese chasing business. And that's how we, as the Brie family, continue to procreate and are able to survive. Your great-great-great-uncle dug the first tunnel in these walls—25 meters long. That's similar to digging a tunnel underneath a 400-meter Olympic running track with only his hands and teeth." On and on it went, the stories of generations of mouse heroics and tragedies.

Then Midas did what he always did and pushed his feelings aside for the greater good of his family. As those feelings continued to compound so did the drive to do what he wanted to do; create art. Every time he picked up a brush, it felt like a natural extension of who he was as a mouse. He just went into the flow of time. He wanted to study the greats like Van Gogh, Degas. Frida Kahlo was his favorite, but there wasn't much time for painting as winter was coming.

Much to Midas's dismay, he continued to play the part of the dutiful son. Autopiloting his way through life. He did what he was supposed to do, and then every night, once the family was fast asleep, he would sneak out into the halls, or use one of his relatives' tunnels, searching for the latest artist installation. There, he would set up his easel and paints. And for hours in the quiet, in the dark, he would replicate the greats.

Midas was on "high alert" because security guard and the museum cat were always a problem. For the most part, he could paint for hours undetected and just flow. Tonight felt different—unlike any other night. There was a full moon and it lit up the gallery with all the new visiting art installations. Once he heard the familiar snore of his sisters and parents, he took a breath, left his bed, went to the secret hole in the wall where he stored all of his art supplies and quietly left his home.

He followed the route that he had mapped out for himself. "Well, at least that's one good thing that I learned from all the cheese chasing adventures," he thought, "it's the best way to get in and out of the museum rooms unnoticed." As he entered the gallery, flooded with moonlight, he saw the print that he was dying to see on the wall. It was of one of his favorite artists he could relate to—Banksy. Nobody knew the identity of Banksy; Midas liked that. If a human could do his work anonymously, why couldn't a mouse do the same?

He stood beneath *The Girl with Balloon* which was released 2004/2005 as a small, limited-edition print; only 150 signed prints and 600 unsigned were released. Of all the artist's works, this is by far his most sought-after.

Midas set up his easel right underneath a skylight that lit up his easel and paints. He took a deep breath, pulled out one of his favorite brushes, and placed the brush on the canvas. Every time Midas began, he could feel energy in the form of liquid love run through his veins. And away he went... Midas, when he had a brush in his hand, felt time was irrelevant. It just faded away into nothingness.

And when he came out of that dreamy love fest powered by artistic revelry, he had a beautiful mouse-sized replication of Banksy's *Girl with Balloon*. He stood back and admired his work. It wasn't exactly like Banksy's; pretty close though.

Deep in introspection, his work, and wishing he'd become the mouse version of Banksy, he didn't hear Pablo creeping in until it was almost too late. The cat's long tail dragged across the top of the security guard's desk at the front of the room, noisily disrupting its contents. Pablo was mid-air and mid-pounce. Fortunately, with Midas' quick thinking and generations of training infused into his DNA he knew that he could escape through a nearby pencil sized hole in the wall. He focused in on the hole and ran as fast as he could in its direction. He made it just in the knick of time, as the cat claws swiped at him missing his body by a hair.

Midas's heart was racing at 700 beats per minute, pounding in his throat. That was just too close of a call. One of too many. Was this really worth it? Yeah, to create the artwork that he wanted to create, it was absolutely worth it. It was worth the sacrifice. It was worth the danger. He loved this latest piece, his replication of his favorite artist, Banksy.

"Oh my God," he thought, "I left the painting and the easel and everything that I had. All my art supplies are there, things I worked so hard for, I accidentally left in the room underneath the painting."

Midas poked his head through the hole to see if the coast was clear, and it wasn't. He pulled his head back, just in time to miss the killer jaws of the ferocious cat. He would have to leave his painting supplies there until the coast was clear. He didn't know when that was going to be.

The next morning, Midas was still in a standoff with the museum cat. He didn't want to leave his supplies. It took him years to scavenge for his stockpile of art supplies but he knew his family would be waking up soon. With an exasperated sigh, Midas left to go back home and chase cheese.

Shortly after Midas left his post, Ann the Museum Docent was making her morning rounds before the museum opened. She had worked at the museum for almost 30 years, loved the morning quiet, and being able to commune with the artwork in silence. Ann's gut instinct for iconic art and artists was so powerful and accurate; she helped discover some of the greatest artists of our time. Many times, her choices were met with a lot of naysaying but Ann's gut always won out in the end.

When she entered the gallery where the new Banksy was housed, Ann sensed there was something different about the energy of the room. Something was "off" but not in a bad way.

She continued to stroll until she was standing 10 feet from *Girl with Balloon,* when her eyes were drawn to the floor and a miniature easel. "That artist's set up looks like it was made for a mouse," Ann thought.

Then she laughed to herself at the ridiculousness of the thought. "Come on, Ann, mice can't paint!" she thought. But as she approached and got closer, she was proven wrong. This piece was not just a replica—it was an interpretation of the artwork and the artist themself, specifically focusing on Banksy's anonymity.

She immediately went over to the security guard, Takysha and asked her to pull the video footage from the Banksy room last night. After reviewing hours of footage, Ann and Tykysha found what they were looking for...there it was, right on video, a small mouse setting up his easel after midnight, working for hours until Pablo disturbed his work. The women silently looked at each other, mouths open and eyes wide in disbelief. They silently replayed the video repeatedly.

Finally, Ann broke their silence, "Yes. Tykysha we are witnessing a mouse artist."

Tykysha said, "I thought I'd seen everything."

"Well, now I have to find that mouse and make it famous."

Tykysha said, "I'd be willing to help you Ann. This is art history."

That night, the women set up the tiny easel and paints. They put out some cheese, locked Pablo Purrcasso in with the Egyptian art, and silently waited for hours.

Finally, as both of them were about to dose off, Midas made his appearance. Due to the strong smell of cheese, he didn't detect the scents of the women. He walked right up to his art supplies and began to pack them away, when Ann began to speak.

"Mr. Mouse, she said. "I will not hurt you. I am here to tell you that I love your artwork and you could be one of the next great artists."

After being on Earth for 65 million years, mice evolved to understand and speak different languages.

"My name is Midas Brie. I come from millions of generations of cheese chasers. I'm not an artist," he said.

Ann said, "I disagree. Your work is beautiful. It's unique and the world needs to experience it. Everyone who gazes upon your artwork will be forever changed for good."

"But how will my family survive without a cheese chaser?" Midas asked.

"If you spend your days painting and creating, I will guarantee food and safety for your family and the generations to come." Midas felt his heart swell and liquid love pour through his veins.

"You mean I get to live my calling? And you're not going to try to change me?" he asked.

"I wouldn't dare try to change you one bit. In fact, you keep being you, and I'll feed you, shelter you and make sure you always have the supplies you need to make great art," Ann replied.

"But no one will believe you." Midas said.

Tykysha jumped in and said, "Yes they will. We'll play the security footage on loop during your first exhibition."

Ann made good on her promises to Midas and the Brie family. The charter for the museum was changed to uphold that promise for as long as the Brie family lived. Midas was able to relax and be himself.

People came from all around the world for hundreds of years to see Midas's work and they were changed for the better. They were inspired to live their dreams—not the stories spoonfed to them by society, family of origin, or cultural conditioning.

THE END

THE MORAL

Follow your heart's calling, don't just do what your family has done for generations. You don't have to do what your parents—or anyone else for that matter—tell you to do.

THREE QUESTIONS

What or who would you need to be, to be your best self?

_____

_____

_____

_____

_____

Who would I need to BE, to be a more artistic human?

_____

_____

_____

_____

Are you living your life's purpose or someone else's?

_____

_____

_____

_____

Black and White Clownfish

BLACK & WHITE CLOWNFISH
Amphiprion ocellaris

Once upon a time, there was a school of common clownfish. They were black and white, happily living together within the tentacles of various anemones. In return for the protection the anemones provided, the clownfish would remove parasites and chase away species that tried to eat its host. It was a beautifully symbiotic relationship that went far deeper than simply host and guest.

They were plankton pickers, meaning they would visually seek and eat plankton and phytoplankton floating in the water column. What was interesting about this group of clownfish, that many other clownfish schools didn't want to talk about, would ignore, rewrite, ban or even worse, erase from the clownfish history is that this species of clownfish changed sex throughout its lifetime.

During this time, a young fish named Greg was born.

Dr. Scale, the fishysician that attended to the birth of Greg, assigned him the sex of male. On the day he was born, Dr. Scale held him up and announced to Greg's mother, "Congratulations! You have a son." His mother was so happy; she had always wanted a son.

Greg loved his family dearly, but as he grew, he felt like an imposter in his own body. He knew what he was supposed to do and what was expected of him, but he never felt at home in his scales.

Greg tried to pretend to be as normal as he could while he fought this out-of-place feeling. Greg awkwardly pretended to agree with his peers when they spoke about things he didn't relate to. He refrained from swimming any other way but straight ahead and in unison with his peers at school.

As Greg grew into a teenager, he began to feel sad and angry about himself. He couldn't control the way that he felt anymore. Greg couldn't pretend anymore. His peers started to make fun of the way that he swam and the way he talked and the things he found interesting. He became withdrawn and wouldn't speak to anyone about what was troubling him.

In an effort to try to help Greg feel better, Greg's mother got him into just about every type of therapy available to them. None of it seemed to help Greg.

Greg was tired of being analyzed. He was tired of being questioned. He was tired of feeling like his body and his soul were not connected.

The only time he was able to self-soothe was during long swims on his own. Greg would swim for hours and hours, exploring every inch of anemones. Usually, he was careful not to venture away too far and kept himself safely hidden from predators, but as he grew more and more troubled he considered disappearing into the blackness of the far beyond.

During one of Greg's long swims, he heard singing coming from a nearby school. He had never heard a song like that before and decided to cautiously get a little closer to have a better look and listen.

He kept himself hidden as the singing grew louder:

Isn't it bliss?
Don't you approve?
One who keeps tearing around
One who can't move
Where are the clowns?
Send in the clowns

Greg sank down deep in the tentacles of the anemone and watched as an orange and white clownfish swam about, changing from male to female and vice versa. He was equally in awe of the happiness of the orange and white clownfish, and the way it changed its body. The orange and white clownfish was equally beautiful and handsome.

Greg shook his head to clear all the confusion from his head and continued to watch this fish in amazement and observed that the fish seemed to be happier as a female. How could he tell? She changed her tune. She began to sing, "Man, I Feel Like a Woman" by Shania Twain. Greg knew the song well. He'd overheard other females in his school singing it as well.

Suddenly, Greg pushed a tiny pebble with his fin that kicked up a cloud of sand. The orange and white clownfish, startled, called out, "Who's there?" Greg knew his cover was blown, and there was no way he could escape without being seen. He sheepishly swam out of the anemone tentacles and mustered up the courage to introduce himself.

He popped his head out and said shyly, "Hey… I'm Greg."

Cautiously looking at him, the fish said, "Hi, I'm Sam. Were you spying on me?"

Greg slowly and carefully got closer to Sam. A little ashamed of himself, Greg said, "I came over because I heard you singing, and it was really quite good, but then I noticed how happy you seemed to be swimming about and transitioning from male to female and back."

Sam, seeming more relaxed now, said, "You could've come up to say hi instead of acting like a creeper."

"You're right. I'm sorry. I didn't mean to give off a predatory vibe. I was just astonished at what I was seeing. I didn't know that was possible."

"Anything is possible," Sam said. "This is actually a part of our nature."

Greg nodded and listened intently as Sam spoke.

"Nothing is really so simple as one or the other in a definite kind of way. Sure, some folks find it in them to be fulfilled just the way they were born. But others, like myself, feel a disconnect from the way we're born versus the way we feel: the way we are truly."

Greg started to feel understood for the first time and began to cry little bubble tears of joy.

Noticing this, Sam said, "There, there Greg. Society isn't always kind to what it doesn't understand. I know how hard it is. I should tell you something about our history. Our ability to transition was given to us by nature to meet the needs of the school. Long ago, fish like us were looked to as special creatures. Our authenticity and freedom were like magic. But magic isn't always understood and sometimes, what isn't understood can inspire envy and jealousy, and then hate. And so, for a long time, fish like us have been forced to hide, and all of our history and validation was carried off into a deep ocean canyon, never to be seen again."

Greg was feeling like something was blossoming in him, but was still confused. "If that's true, then how do you know all of this?"

"Because we've always been here," Sam said. "We've shared our history in our communities so that it lives on in our spirits. Someone told me, and now I am telling you. And so now that you know, how are you feeling?"

And for the first time, Greg felt great. Greg felt seen and heard and made whole. "I feel amazing," Greg said. "I've got to start living my life the way it was meant to be lived."

Sam smiled, "I can't promise that it will be easy for your family or peers to understand you, but you will be free. When you're ready, why don't you come to dinner over at the Red Rock Social Club. I'll be there and there will be others you can talk to."

"I would love that," Greg said. "I've got to be honest. Before I heard your song, I was considering swimming far off from home and disappearing forever. I am so thankful for you."

Sam took Greg's fins in her fins and said, "Everything is going to be different now. I promise you."

THE END

THE MORAL

People of historically marginalized groups want to be free to live their lives in peace and in a way that honors them.

Author's Note: *Clownfish change sex and, while some folks in the trans community undergo sex changes, it is not exclusive. A clownfish changes sex as a result of an evolutionary survival function. Our gender identity isn't the same.*

According to the Human Rights Campaign (HRC), gender identity is defined as: One's innermost concept of self as male, female, a blend of both or neither – how individuals perceive themselves and what they call themselves. One's gender identity can be the same or different from their sex assigned at birth.

THREE QUESTIONS

What does it mean to be transgender?

_____

_____

_____

_____

_____

How does someone know they're transgender?

_____

_____

_____

_____

_____

What's the difference between sexual orientation and gender identity?

_____

_____

_____

_____

_____

Conclusion

This book is meant to explore the natural world as an example of what's possible:

1. Forging your own path has the potential to save your life.

2. Fathers want to be part of their children's lives. Instituting paternity leave has far-reaching benefits.

3. Burnout has become an epidemic. The American Institute of Stress found that 75% of all doctors visits are stress related. Burnout can have serious consequences for both employees and employers. According to a study by the *Harvard Business Review*, burnout costs American businesses $300 billion per year.

4. Gossip can damage lives. Some negative consequences of workplace gossip are:

    - Erosion of trust and morale.

    - Lost productivity and wasted time.

    - Increased anxiety among employees, as rumors circulate without clear information as to what is and isn't fact.

    - Divisiveness among employees as people take sides.

    - Hurt feelings and reputations.

    - Attrition due to good employees leaving the company because of an unhealthy work environment.

5. Taking a holistic approach to diversity, equity, inclusion, and accessibility can drive revenue, innovation, and growth, to create a psychologically safe space for people to thrive at work.

6. Trying to make people conform removes their unique magical essence.

7. Money can't buy everything.

8. According to RAINN, "Consent is an agreement between participants to engage in sexual activity. Consent should be clearly and freely communicated. A verbal and affirmative expression of consent can help both you and your partner to understand and respect each other's boundaries."

9. Follow your heart's calling, don't just do what your family has done for generations. You don't have to do what your parents—or anyone else for that matter—tell you to do.

10. People of historically marginalized communities want to be free to live their lives in peace and in a way that honors them.

I challenge you, dear reader, to take a look deep inside yourself and ask: "Am I living up to my highest potential as a human being?" Be honest. The only way true transformation can take shape is if you're honest with yourself. If the answer is no, ask yourself, "What do I need to shift and change inside me to get the result I want?" Then take action. One baby step at a time toward change can end up in a marathon's worth of results.

You can change the world by changing yourself. If these fables resonate with you, practice embodying and enacting the lessons you learned throughout the book, one at a time, and watch the world transform in front of your eyes.

I'd love to hear from you about your experience with these fables. If you're moved to, share your thoughts, comments, and feedback with me by sending me an email at kelly@youloudandclear.com.

Thanks for reading my work. I appreciate you and your unique energy. Make it a great life.

www.ingramcontent.com/pod-product-compliance
Lightning Source LLC
Chambersburg PA
CBHW051325120626
46547CB00015B/2407